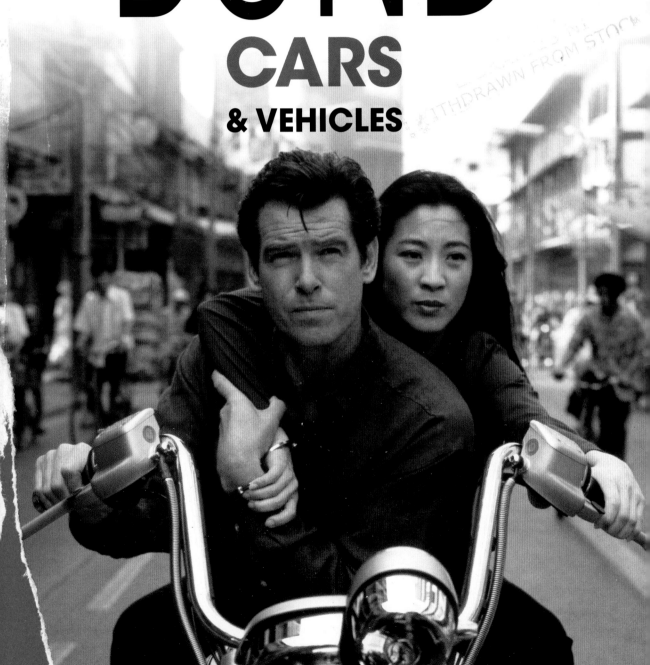

BOND

CARS

& VEHICLES

BOND

CARS

& VEHICLES

Alastair Dougall

CONTENTS

Dr. No™

Bond goes hunting in the Caribbean for SPECTRE's Dr. No, who is suspected of "toppling" US spacecraft. As soon as Bond arrives in Jamaica he is targeted by Dr. No's assassins, including the hearse-driving Three Blind Mice. Bond and his CIA ally Quarrel sail to Dr. No's private island, Crab Key, where they battle his Dragon Tank. Quarrel is killed, but Bond survives to destroy Dr. No and his organization.

Ahoy, Mr Bond. Ahoy, Mr Bond.
Well, well. What's the matter? Do you need help?
I'm quite sure you don't!
Well, now that you're here, you'd better give us a tow.

Leiter and Bond

The black hearse containing the Three Blind Mice was lying in wait, concealed among trees, as Bond drove past in his blue Sunbeam.

The twisting, dusty mountain roads of Jamaica are no place for reckless drivers. Bond was on his way to an assignation with seductive Government House secretary Miss Taro when his Sunbeam Alpine was pursued by the Three Blind Mice killers. Dr. No's gang of Jamaican assassins was about to be further depleted.

BLUE MOUNTAIN BREAKDOWN

A crane blocked the road. Bond's smaller, more manoeuvrable vehicle dodged beneath the crane's arm. The bulky hearse swerved, crashed down a steep incline, and burst into flames.

I think they were on their way to a funeral.

Bond

DRAGON TANK

"Stay where you are," ordered a voice through a megaphone. Bond and Honey had no hope of escape as Dr. No's dragon tank lumbered towards them.

A roaring gush of flame announced the arrival of the dragon of Crab Key, so feared by local fishermen. Bond realized at once that diesel engines powered this dragon. Quarrel, bravely trying to shoot at the vehicle's driver, was incinerated. Bond and Honey had little choice but to surrender to Dr. No's guards.

Okay Captain, if that's not a dragon, what is it?

Quarrel

Dr. No's guards wore special suits, indicating that the island had abnormally high radiation levels. They handcuffed Bond and dragged him away, forcing Honey to follow.

FROM RUSSIA WITH LOVE

SPECTRE baits a trap for Bond and MI6 with a beautiful Russian defector, Tatiana "Tania" Romanova and a secret decoding machine. Bond and Tania, posing as newlyweds on honeymoon, escape from Istanbul with the decoder on the Orient Express. They have little time for romance as SPECTRE's deadly web entangles them.

RUNNING FOR COVER

I'd say one of their aircraft is missing.

Bond

Bond seized his folding AR-7 sniper's rifle from his standard-issue attaché case. As SPECTRE's helicopter roared overhead, he took out the co-pilot, whose grenade exploded inside the cockpit.

SPECTRE's top assassin, Grant, was dead, killed by Bond on the Orient Express. The Lektor decoder was in Bond's grasp and Tania Romanova was at his side. To confuse pursuers, Bond used Grant's escape route, hijacking a lorry. The plan worked, until a heavily-armed helicopter announced that SPECTRE had abandoned subtlety in favour of direct action.

Morzeny's goons were armed with rifle grenades and machine guns. Bond knew that desperate measures were needed.

Bond and Tania were keeping to Red Grant's escape agenda, heading for Venice in a powerboat, when SPECTRE made yet another attempt on their lives. This time, top enforcer Morzeny led a trio of boats against them.

SPEEDBOAT ESCAPE

Bullets punctured fuel drums aboard Bond's boat. Bond released the drums and ignited the spilt fuel with a Verey pistol. A wall of fire incinerated Morzeny and his men.

GOLDFINGER ™

Bond is assigned to investigate suspected gold smuggler Auric Goldfinger. To trail Goldfinger's vintage Rolls-Royce, Q Branch brings Bond's field equipment bang up to date with the finest available British sports car: an Aston Martin DB5. Q equips the DB5 with an arsenal of gadgets and defence systems, hoping that Bond will return the vehicle intact at the end of the assignment. Unfortunately, the Goldfinger mission proves tougher than expected.

Where's my Bentley?
Oh, it's had its day, I'm afraid.
But it's never let me down.
M's orders, Double-O-Seven.
You'll be using this Aston
Martin DB5 with modifications.

Bond and Q

ASTON MARTIN DB5

Bond was initially disappointed when MI6 replaced his
Bentley Mk IV with an Aston Martin DB5, but he soon changed
his mind. He damaged the car in a chase with Goldfinger's
henchmen, but was back behind the wheel for his Thunderball
mission. The DB5's rakish good looks, adroit handling and
punchy performance mirrored Bond's devil-may-care attitude to
life, and his 1964 silver-grey Aston Martin DB5 remained his
favourite car for personal use.

Just some of the DB5's modifications: front view shows machine guns, bumper rams and revolving number plates. Rear view shows revolving plates, tyre scythe, bulletproof screen, caltrop dispensers, oil-jet pipe, smoke-screen pipe and rear bumper rams.

Engine capacity: 3995 cc **Max. speed:** 145.2 mph (232.3 km/h) **Acceleration:** 0-60 mph (0-96 km/h) in 7.1 secs **Length:** 4.6 m (15 ft) **Width:** 1.7 m (5 ft 6 in) **Modifications:** front-wing 7.6 mm machine guns; dashboard moving-map display linked to magnetic homer; tracking signal receiver in side mirror; bulletproof windows and windscreen; rear bulletproof shield; oil-slick dispenser and caltrop dispenser behind rear lights; front and rear hydraulic ramming bumpers; passenger ejector seat; smoke screen from exhaust pipe; tyre scythe in rear wheel hub; revolving number plates; gun drawer under driver's seat; radio telephone.

Goldfinger's magnificent 1937 Rolls-Royce Phantom III suited the industrialist's grandiose personality. The car's yellow paint job hinted at its owner's main predilection: gold. After defeating Goldfinger on the golf course, Bond placed a homing device in the Rolls' boot so he could follow the car unseen in his Aston Martin DB5.

THE GOLD ROLLS-ROYCE

She's a beauty. Phantom 337, isn't she? **You are a clever, resourceful man, Mr. Bond.** Why, thank you. **Perhaps too clever. This is the second time our paths have crossed. Let's leave it at that.**

Bond and **Goldfinger**

Bond discovered the secret of Goldfinger's smuggling racket at his factory in Switzerland. The Rolls-Royce's bodywork was 24-carat gold.

THUNDERBALL ™

Once again, Bond takes on the might of SPECTRE, which has hijacked two atomic bombs and is holding the US and UK to ransom. Bond leaves his DB5 in Europe to travel to the Bahamas and lock horns with Emilio Largo, SPECTRE's Number Two. Largo's yacht is crucial to the bomb plot, and Bond's intervention guarantees an explosive conclusion.

CAR WASH

Bond's DB5 proved its mettle in a brief battle with SPECTRE agents in France. Colonel Jacques Boitier, a prominent SPECTRE agent, had faked his death then posed as his own grieving widow at the funeral. Bond saw through the deception and, after a brutal struggle, killed Boitier at a chateau. Cornered by Boitier's men, Bond donned a jet pack to soar over the walls to where his Aston Martin and agent La Porte were waiting.

The Bell-Textron jet pack was perfect for a quick getaway.

Bond's response to enemy gunfire was to raise the DB5's bulletproof shield, then utilize Q's new gadget: high-pressure water jets.

LIGHTNING FLASH

Fiona Volpe's bike was equipped with four front-firing rockets. Count Lippe paid the ultimate price for failing to eliminate Bond.

Shot at by SPECTRE agent Count Lippe driving a Ford Skyliner, Bond prepared to take appropriate defensive measures. In his rear-view mirror, he spotted a motorcyclist riding a BSA A65L Lightning. The lone biker was SPECTRE assassin Fiona Volpe.

Number Two has done well—unlike Count Lippe... Send a message to the Execution Branch.

Ernst Stavro Blofeld,
SPECTRE Number One

DISCO VOLANTE

Emilio Largo, SPECTRE's Number Two, was proud of his magnificent motor yacht. He told Bond the *Disco Volante* could do 20 knots. What he didn't tell Bond was that its hull was equipped with doors, allowing large items to be loaded unseen. Largo also omitted to mention that the *Disco* could go a great deal faster than 20 knots, was armed with a smoke pod and an anti-aircraft gun and had a stolen atom bomb on board.

Largo and Bond fought to the death as the *Disco Volante* veered out of control towards coral reefs.

Confronted by US warships, Largo jettisoned the yacht's cocoon. The *Disco* became a hydrofoil capable of 70 knots. Largo would have escaped with an atom bomb, but Bond clambered aboard to foil his and SPECTRE's plans.

YOU ONLY LIVE TWICE

An unknown party, operating from somewhere in Japan, is hijacking spacecraft belonging to the US and Soviet Union. M sends Bond to Japan to investigate. Agent Aki and Tiger Tanaka of the Japanese Secret Service get Bond out of some tight corners, and Q brings the Little Nellie gyrocopter to help Bond locate the enemy base. Bond discovers that SPECTRE is plotting to foment war between East and West and finally meets SPECTRE's Number One: Ernst Stavro Blofeld.

Ah, welcome to Japan, Dad. Is my little girl hot and ready? Look, Double-O-Seven, I've had a long and tiring journey, probably to no purpose, and I'm in no mood for your juvenile quips.

Bond and Q

We are being chased by gunmen in black sedan... arrange usual reception, please.

Aki to Tiger Tanaka

The enemy Toyota dangled from the helicopter's magnet. Osato's assassins tried to jump out but were soon too high up.

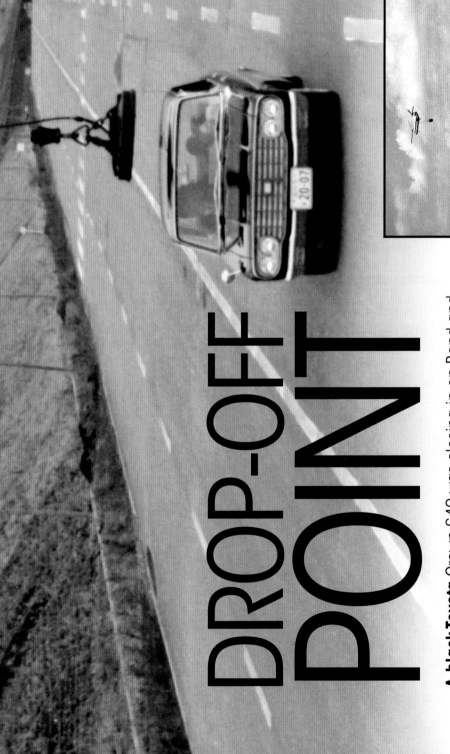

DROP-OFF POINT

A black Toyota Crown S40 was closing in on Bond and Japanese agent Aki's Toyota 2000GT. It was full of gunmen with orders to kill from Mr. Osato, whose business empire, Bond suspected, was backing attacks on US and Soviet spacecraft. Aki radioed her boss, Tiger Tanaka, who disposed of the threat in spectacular fashion.

The Japanese Secret Service's Kawasaki helicopter flew the gunmen's car over Tokyo Bay. The magnet was shut off and the vehicle dropped like a stone.

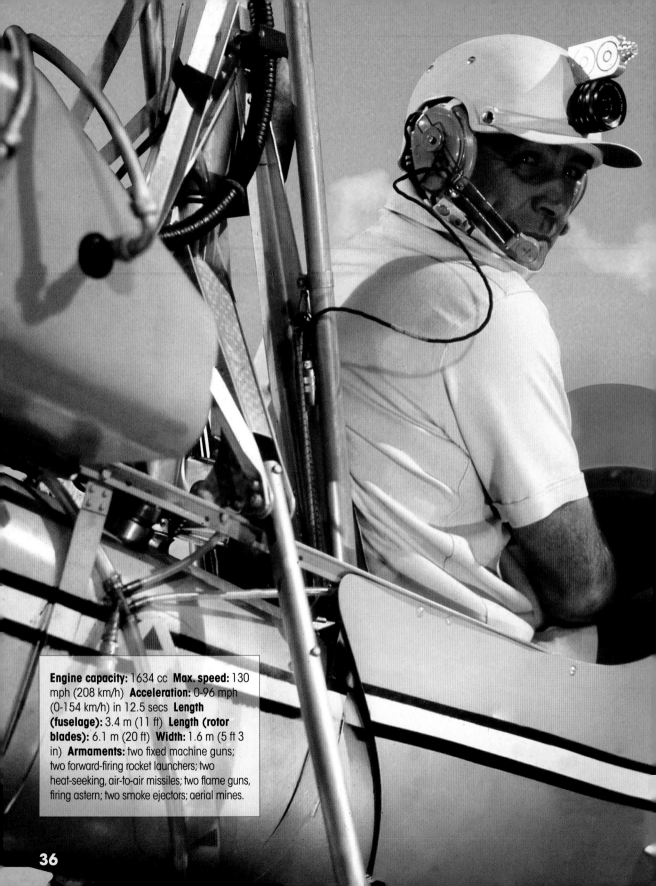

Engine capacity: 1634 cc **Max. speed:** 130 mph (208 km/h) **Acceleration:** 0-96 mph (0-154 km/h) in 12.5 secs **Length (fuselage):** 3.4 m (11 ft) **Length (rotor blades):** 6.1 m (20 ft) **Width:** 1.6 m (5 ft 3 in) **Armaments:** two fixed machine guns; two forward-firing rocket launchers; two heat-seeking, air-to-air missiles; two flame guns, firing astern; two smoke ejectors; aerial mines.

LITTLE NELLIE

A **helmet** equipped with a cine-camera sent pictures of Matsu Island's volcanic terrain back to base.

What's Little Nellie?
Oh, she's a wonderful girl. Very small. Very Fast. Can do anything. Just your type.

Tiger Tanaka and **Bond**

Q grumbled about supplying Bond "in the field", but he was proud of his Little Nellie autogyro. Her parts could be transported in four trunks. Quickly assembled, she was ideal for surveillance missions over upland regions. And although Little Nellie looked frail, she was sturdy, fast, manoeuvrable and exceptionally well-armed.

Q Branch had made "one or two improvements" since Bond had last flown Little Nellie. Her weaponry had been considerably augmented.

37

ON HER MAJESTY'S SECRET SERVICE™

Bond impersonates a heraldry expert to infiltrate the alpine clinic of the "Comte de Bleuchamp". Blofeld is making a belated bid for respectability and threatens to loose his Angels of Death upon the world if his wish is not granted. Bond, assisted by gang boss Draco, stages a frontal attack to crush Blofeld and rescue Tracy di Vicenzo, Draco's daughter – and Bond's fiancée.

I think some people don't know we're crusaders.

Draco

BOND TO THE RESCUE

Bond threw off his jacket and plunged after the girl. She did not resist when he carried her from the waves. Her name was Teresa di Vicenzo.

As Bond fought off a sudden attack by two men, the girl jumped into Bond's DBS, drove to her own Mercury Cougar, and took off.

Bond was driving the latest model Aston Martin, the DBS, near a beach in Portugal when he caught sight of a beautiful girl in a flowing dress walking straight into the sea. Bond was about to meet his future wife.

FAST TRACK

Bond had escaped Blofeld's clinic and was hiding among the crowd at a ski resort, but he knew it was only a matter of time before Blofeld's henchmen pounced. Bond needed a miracle – and one appeared: Tracy di Vicenzo on ice skates. She took Bond for a breakneck ride in her Mercury Cougar, joining a stock-car race to shake off Blofeld's gang.

A blizzard made driving impossible, forcing Tracy and Bond to spend the night in a barn. They were safe – for a while.

Looks like we've hit the rush hour!
Bond

Diamonds Are Forever ™

Bond penetrates a diamond-smuggling pipeline that leads him to alluring, light-fingered Tiffany Case, Las Vegas and, ultimately, Ernst Stavro Blofeld of SPECTRE, apparently back from the dead. Bond steals a moonbuggy and gives Tiffany the ride of her life on the way to destroying Blofeld's diamond-studded bid for world domination.

Listen, you can drop me off at the next corner.
This whole thing is getting a little out of hand!

Tiffany Case

MOONBUGGY
ESCAPE

The trail of smuggled diamonds led Bond to WWTectronics, an aerospace complex. After impersonating a technician, Bond had to make a quick getaway, seizing the first available machine – a moonbuggy. Capable of 80 mph (129 km/h), the buggy was ideal for the desert terrain surrounding the complex, leaving WWTectronics security's squad cars floundering in the dust.

The moonbuggy was standing on a realistic stage set, constructed to resemble the moon. Dressed as astronaut explorers, the technicians were too slow to prevent Bond's escape.

Bond abandoned the moonbuggy and completed his escape on an all-terrain Honda ATC three-wheeler bike.

WILD RIDE

Eluding WWTectronics security was one thing, escaping the Las Vegas Police Department on its own turf was quite another. But there was no stopping Bond once he got behind the wheel of Tiffany Case's red Ford Mustang Mach I. The resultant damage to the LVPD's police cruisers was entirely of the officers' own making.

There goes the sonovabitchin' saboteur!
Las Vegas Police Sheriff

Bond led the police cruisers into a car park, then found his own way out, vaulting over parked vehicles.

LIVE AND LET DIE ™

The deaths of three agents send Bond to Harlem and the Caribbean isle of San Monique. Bond spirits away beautiful fortune-teller Solitaire and dodges hoodlums on the Louisiana bayou before smashing a voodoo-driven heroin operation run by San Monique's evil president, Dr. Kananga.

That's the car. They must have gone inside. Pull up where you can. Sure hope you make friends easy.

Bond and Cab Driver

DANGER: LOW BRIDGE

Dr. Kananga contacted San Monique's police force as soon as he realized Bond and Solitaire had escaped and were on the run. Bond had to get Solitaire to the coast, where a boat waited to carry them to New Orleans. He decided to go by bus.

The Routemaster smashed into a low bridge. The top deck neatly sheared off, confounding the pursuing motorcycle cops. Bond then drove to San Monique harbour, with Solitaire still holding on tight.

Bond gave Adam, one of Mr. Big's enforcers, more than a run for his money, despite having the slower boat.

What the...?!

Sheriff J. W. Pepper

Pursued by Mr. Big's thugs, Bond made waves on the Louisiana bayou in a Glastron GT-150 speedboat. Mr. Big's henchmen were close behind and a thrilling chase began, a chase that did not go unobserved by County Sheriff J. W. Pepper and the State Police.

BAYOU BURN-UP

Bond took a short cut through an outdoor wedding. His pursuer's steering was not in Bond's class and he ploughed into the cake – to the bride's dismay.

THE MAN WITH THE GOLDEN GUN™

A gold bullet inscribed "007" looks like the clearest possible threat by Scaramanga, the world's deadliest assassin. Bond's pursuit of the Man with the Golden Gun takes him speeding along the waterways of Thailand and chasing a flying car. He finally runs Scaramanga to earth on his private island for a fun house duel to the death.

A GIANT LEAP

Scaramanga had kidnapped MI6 agent Mary Goodnight, who had the invaluable Solex Agitator in her possession. In a flash, Bond ran to a car showroom and jumped behind the wheel of a new, red AMC Hornet X. He then accelerated through the showroom window – to the astonishment of the vehicle's potential buyer, Sheriff J. W. Pepper.

A klong waterway separated Bond from Scaramanga, but not for long. Bond used a collapsed bridge as a ramp to send the Hornet soaring across to the other bank.

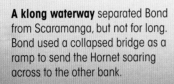

Hidden doors opened, and Scaramanga was free as a bird, heading for his private island.

So, if I heard correctly, Scaramanga got clean away.
Yes, sir.
A car that sprouted wings... and Miss Goodnight was in the boot!

M and **Bond**

THE FLYING CAR

Bond and Sheriff J. W. Pepper followed the AMC Matador containing Scaramanga and his sidekick Nick Nack as it vanished inside a hangar. Scaramanga seemed to have been cornered at last. Then, to Bond and Pepper's astonishment, Scaramanga's car took wing.

TH SP WH L V D M ™

Shipping magnate Karl Stromberg is suspected of involvement in the hijacking of British and Soviet nuclear submarines. Bond and top KGB agent Major Anya Amasova reconnoitre Stromberg's offshore base, *Atlantis*, in a very special, amphibious Lotus Esprit S1, courtesy of Q Branch. They encounter fierce resistance, but Bond and Anya's real battles with Stromberg's forces lie ahead – aboard the power-mad tycoon's supertanker *Liparus*.

Ever get the feeling someone doesn't like you?

Bond

WET NELLIE

Pursued in his Lotus Esprit SI by Stromberg's henchmen, including his pilot Naomi in her helicopter gunship, Bond took evasive action: he plunged off a jetty into the sea. Naomi assumed Bond had crashed but, with the flick of a few switches, he quickly converted the Lotus into a mini-sub. Bond took revenge on his circling assailant with a well-aimed missile, then he and his passenger, Major Anya Amasova, inspected Stromberg's *Atlantis* base.

Engine capacity: 1,973 cc **Max. speed:** 138 mph (221 km/h) **Acceleration:** 0-60 mph (0-96 km/h) in 6.8 secs **Length:** 4.2 m (13 ft 9 in) **Width:** 1.85 m (6 ft 1 in) **Diving depth:** 100 m (328 ft) **Modifications:** cement sprayer; front-firing torpedoes; rear ink jet; mine launcher in chassis; missile launcher in rear hatch; bulletproof windows; periscope in roof; full amphibious conversion, including propeller assembly in rear bumper.

Hunted by Stromberg's underwater assassins, Wet Nellie confused pursuers with ink and hit back with a torpedo.

LIPARUS

Stromberg's secret weapon in his war against the surface world was his supertanker *Liparus*. A unique submarine tracking system, devised by Stromberg's scientists, forced a sub to the surface, then the tanker's specially designed bows opened to swallow the vessel. The *Liparus'* hold had room for three submarines, whose crews were imprisoned in holding pens. The USS *Wayne,* with Bond on board, was the *Liparus'* third and final victim.

Stromberg's plan to cause nuclear armageddon with missiles fired by the captured nuclear subs HMS *Ranger* and *Potemkin* was near fruition. Unless Bond acted swiftly.

Commander, you have precisely two minutes to open your hatches and surrender your ship. The alternative is extermination – by cyanide gas.

Stromberg

MOONRAKER™

Bond investigates aerospace tycoon Hugo Drax, maker of a Moonraker space shuttle that has mysteriously vanished. Teaming up with the CIA's Dr. Holly Goodhead, Bond travels to South America, battles Jaws on a cable car and a jungle river, and discovers Drax's launch site for his scheme to repopulate the Earth with his own beautiful people.

You delivered a shuttle to the US government. Then you hijacked it. Why?
I needed it... Now you have distracted me enough.

THE BONDOLA

Hugo Drax was determined to put a stop to Bond's enquiries in Venice. He arranged a series of assassination attempts – surely one of them had to succeed. Bond seemed to be a sitting duck as he took a leisurely ride on the canals. But his gondola had modifications that made it surprisingly difficult to catch.

Concealed control panels transformed Bond's gondola into a speedboat and then a hovercraft as he dodged Drax's killers.

Pigeons scattered and people looked on in amazement as Bond took a short cut across St. Mark's Square.

Bond travelled up river in a Glastron/Carlson CV-23HT speedboat. It was modified to discourage pursuit with a stern mine and torpedo launcher and a bulletproof shield. Bond soon needed them as Jaws and Drax's henchmen gave chase.

WATERFALL LEAP

A phial Bond removed from Drax's Venice glass factory contained a nerve gas derived from a rare orchid. Q had a boat ("If Double-O-Seven can be trusted to look after it") to take Bond to the Tapirapé river region, deep in the South American jungle, where the orchid was exclusively found. Bond didn't know it, but he and Jaws were heading for another fall.

As Bond sped towards a waterfall, he baled out in style using an on-board hang-glider. Lacking this refinement, Jaws' boat went over the falls with Jaws still in it. But if Bond thought he had shaken Jaws off for good, he was mistaken.

FOR YOUR EYES ONLY ™

Bond goes hunting for a missing ATAC device, used for ordering the launch of British Polaris missiles. He is not alone, encountering vengeful, crossbow-wielding Melina Havelock, and Greek smugglers Kristatos and Colombo. One of these smugglers arranged her parents' assassination and is in league with the KGB. But which?

Sir, the man we want is Emile Leopold Locque... The Italian Secret Service think that at this moment he is in Cortina.
I'll instruct Ferrara, our man in northern Italy to contact you there... And Double-O-Seven: try not to muck it up again!

Bond and **Tanner**,
MI6 Chief of Staff

A smack with his machine pistol – and boom! – one dead henchman and another Bond car write-off. Would Q regret fitting that burglar protection system to Bond's Lotus?

Captured in Spain by hitman Gonzales' men, there seemed no way out for Bond – until a crossbow bolt buried itself in Gonzales' back. Bond broke free and came face to face with the archer, Melina Havelock. Bond and Melina shook off two Peugeot pursuit cars in her indestructible Citröen 2CV, barrelling down lanes, lurching through a sleepy village, and literally flying through olive groves.

A DRIVE
in the COUNTRY

OCTOPUSSY™

Fresh from piloting the Acrostar minijet on a mission in Latin America, Bond dodges danger in a Delhi tuk-tuk chasing stolen Russian art treasures. He uncovers a highly explosive conspiracy involving a sleazy Afghan prince, a warmongering Soviet general and the superb Octopussy, with her Floating Palace, her exotic barge and her travelling circus,

THE ACROSTAR

Ground troops fired a Rapier surface-to-air missile at the Acrostar. Bond dodged through the spy plane's hangar, and the missile did his work for him.

Bond's cunning attempt to impersonate an army officer and sabotage a spy plane had hit trouble. He was saved by his quick-thinking assistant Bianca, who artfully distracted his guards, and by the acrobatic Acrostar. Once at the minijet's controls, Bond effortlessly snatched victory from defeat.

Bianca transported the Acrostar in a horse box, attracting little attention as a horse trials was taking place near the base.

Fill her up, please!
Bond

Max. level speed: 320 mph (512 km/h)
Ceiling: 9,000 m (30,000 ft) **Wingspan:** 3.9
m (13 ft) **Length:** 3.6 m (12 ft) **Height:** 1.7
m (5 ft 8 in) **Weight:** 204.5 kg (450 lb).

TUK-TUK TAXI RIDE

Khan's henchmen's jeep chased the tuk-tuk through a bustling street market.

Exiled Afghan prince Kamal Khan was a sore loser – as Bond quickly discovered when he outswindled him at backgammon. Khan's assassins rampaged through the Delhi streets after Bond's tuk-tuk taxi. Fortunately the tuk-tuk's driver, local MI6 agent Vijay, knew his way around, and also how to get the best out of the little vehicle. He even invented his own version of a flyover.

A VIEW TO A KILL ™

Industrialist Max Zorin has a ruthlessly simple plan to corner the microchip market: wipe California's Silicon Valley off the map. Bond unravels the devious, murderous schemes of the psychotic Zorin and his assassin partner May Day, leading to a final battle on his airship, swaying and swinging above the Golden Gate Bridge.

This'll hurt him more than me.

Max Zorin

Bond was sure he had the assassin cornered, then he – or she – leapt into space.

TAXI FOR BOND

The mysterious, black-clad killer parachuted from the Eiffel Tower, but Bond refused to give up the chase. He hailed a Renault taxi, ejected the driver, and drove the car to destruction though the streets of Paris.

Taxi – follow that parachute!

Bond

A crash barrier proved no obstacle to Bond's progress.

You lost, Double-O-Seven.
It was a mistake to kill Tibbett.
I'm about to make the same
mistake twice.

Max Zorin and **Bond**

Bond galloped up to the Rolls
on his all-too-fiery steed, hoping
for a smooth getaway.

A SINKING FEELING

Bond exchanged one hellish experience for another when he leapt from his crazed, doped horse, Inferno, into his Rolls-Royce Silver Cloud. May Day was at the wheel, and Bond's trusty colleague and acting chauffeur Sir Godfrey Tibbett was dead in the back seat. A little while later, Bond was fighting for breath and facing a watery grave.

Zorin and May Day waited until they were quite sure Bond had drowned in the lake. The air in one of the Rolls' tyres saved Bond's life.

Zorin watched helplessly as his plan to explode a bomb in his flooded mine and cause an earthquake misfired. Seeing a chance for revenge, Zorin swooped low to snatch up Bond's ally, geologist Stacey Sutton.

EXPLOSIVE FINALE

If Zorin couldn't destroy half of California, he'd have his crazy fun. Capturing Stacey Sutton would be a start, especially with Bond swinging on his airship's mooring rope. But then Bond spoiled things by tethering the airship to the Golden Gate Bridge, and Zorin's "father", ex-Nazi geneticist Dr. Carl Mortner, made the fatal mistake of playing with dynamite in the cabin...

THE LIVING DAYLIGHTS ™

Bond goes behind the Iron Curtain to search for cello virtuoso and amateur sniper Kara Milovy. He believes she could hold the key to a campaign to murder MI6 agents allegedly orchestrated by the KGB. Bond needs to move fast to bring her to the West – and Q provides the wheels.

Just taking the Aston Martin out for a spin, Q.
Be careful, Double-O-Seven. It's just had a new coat of paint!

Bond and Q

BREAK FOR THE
BORDER

Q had "winterized" Bond's new Aston Martin V8 with spiked tyres and outriggers to ensure good handling in the iciest conditions. With its formidable speed and weaponry, the V8 proved the perfect vehicle to outrun the police, out-gun border patrols and bring Kara Milovy home free.

Engine capacity: 5,340 cc; fuel injection
Max. speed: 146 mph (248 km/h)
Acceleration: 0-60 mph (0-96 km/h) in 6.6 secs **Length:** 4.67 m (15 ft 4 in)
Width: 1.83 m (6 ft) **Modifications:** hard top; retractable outriggers; ice tyres; police-band radio; rear jet engine booster rocket; twin heat-seeking missile launchers; front hubcap laser beams.

Outriggers deployed, Bond's V8 soared over the astonished Czech border guards.

Brace yourself!
Bond

LICENCE TO KILL ™

Bond and the DEA's Felix Leiter capture drug baron Franz Sanchez in Florida. The gang boss escapes and his men mutilate Leiter and murder his bride. Acting without MI6 sanction, Bond wages a one-man war of vengeance on Sanchez's merciless empire, culminating in the destruction of his fleet of drug-transporting tankers.

You disappoint me. Who are you working for? Huh? Tell me!

Sanchez to Bond

LEITER'S
WEDDING DAY

Leiter and Bond pursued Sanchez's light plane in a helicopter. Sanchez seemed sure to escape, but Bond had an audacious plan.

What the hell are you doing?
Let's go fishing!

Leiter and **Bond**

The day dawned sunny and bright for Felix Leiter's Florida wedding. But as he and his best man, James Bond, drove to the church, word came from the DEA that one of America's Most Wanted, Latin American drug tsar Franz Sanchez, had been spotted in the area. The wedding might have to wait.

Lowered onto the tail of Sanchez's aircraft, Bond secured a line to it. The "fish" caught, Bond and Leiter parachuted down to the church on time.

Pam revealed her flying expertise as she brought the Piper PA-18 Super Cub to within a few feet of the tanker. Bond prepared to jump.

Bond had laid waste to Sanchez's cocaine labs. Now he set about finishing what he'd started. Ex-CIA pilot Pam Bouvier enabled him to leap onto one of Sanchez's fleet of four Kenworth W900B tankers. Each tanker was loaded with a highly combustible blend of cocaine and gasoline – one of Sanchez's favoured methods of smuggling his drugs into the US.

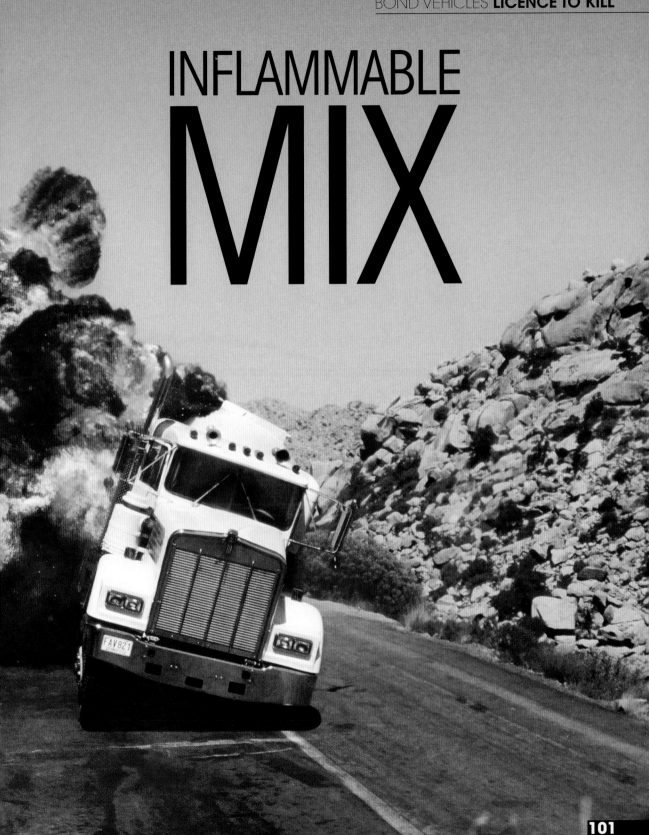

INFLAMMABLE
MIX

GOLDENEYE™

A long-ago mission in Siberia, during which his friend, MI6 agent Alec Trevelyan, was captured and shot, comes back to haunt Bond. An encounter with a red Ferrari alerts Bond to the Janus crime syndicate, led by a familiar, if disfigured, face. Janus steals the GoldenEye weapons system, and Bond needs help from resourceful Russian computer programmer Natalya Simonova to save Britain from devastation and economic meltdown.

Do you destroy every vehicle you get into? **Standard operating procedure.**

Natalya Simonova
and **Bond**

DANGEROUS CURVES

The Ferrari's driver was a femme fatale named Xenia Onatopp, an ex-Soviet fighter pilot with links to the Janus organization.

Bond disliked being evaluated by MI6. A woman driving a red Ferrari provided a welcome distraction, overtaking his Aston Martin DB5 with a mocking wave. Bond took up the challenge – and noticed that the Ferrari had false number plates.

Bond's Aston Martin and the Ferrari Spider 355 GTS caused consternation among a group of cyclists.

James – is it really necessary to drive so fast?
More often than you'd think.
MI6 evaluator Caroline and **Bond**

MI6 training enabled Bond to drive virtually any vehicle. Busting out of the KGB's St. Petersburg headquarters, he hijacked a Russian T-80BV tank. The car carrying Janus' General Ourumov and Natalya Simonova, innocent witness of the General's crimes, had to be caught. Bond didn't care how much damage the 46-ton tank did in the process.

Seeing Natalya brought aboard an armoured train, Bond positioned the tank on the railway tracks and waited.

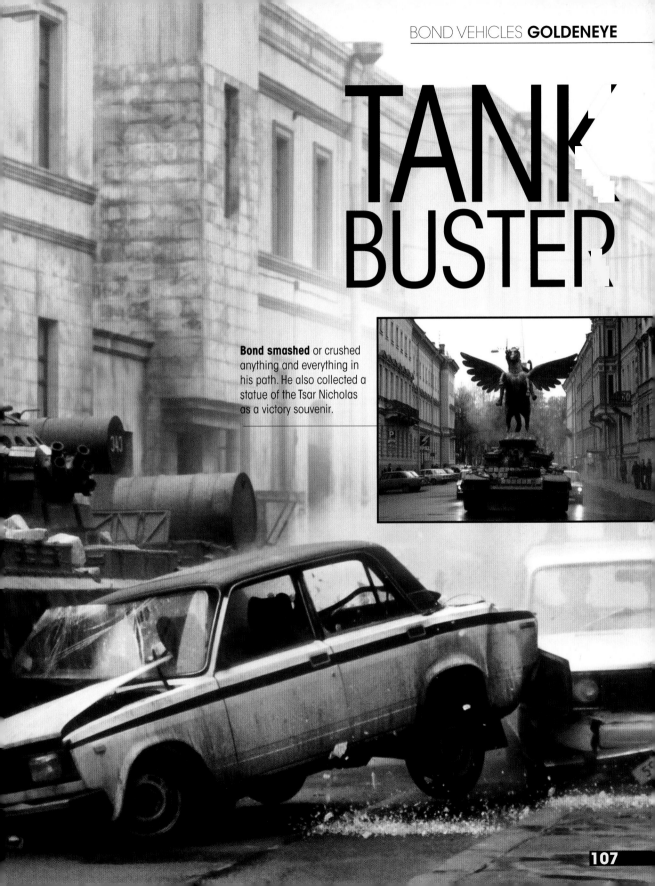

TANK
BUSTER

Bond smashed or crushed anything and everything in his path. He also collected a statue of the Tsar Nicholas as a victory souvenir.

Trevelyan and his sidekick Xenia Onatopp took off from the wrecked train in a helicopter concealed in a truck.

DEATH TRAIN

Bond and Natalya escaped
the train seconds before
Trevelyan's bomb went off.

One of Janus' bases was a decommissioned
armoured train formerly used for transporting
missiles. Bond used a hijacked tank to derail
the locomotive, hoping to rescue Natalya
Simonova. Janus' scarred leader, Bond's
former MI6 friend Alec Trevelyan, tried to turn
the train into Bond and Natalya's tomb. They
had three minutes to get out.

Bond. Only Bond.
He's going to derail us.
Trevelyan and **Onatopp**

TomorrowNeverDies ™

M suspects press baron Elliot Carver's news agency of collusion in the sinking of a British warship: Bond's enquiries into Carver's organization are met with ruthless violence. Q's customized BMW gets Bond out of one tight corner, but only Bond's own never-say-die resourcefulness keeps him in the hunt. That, and a little help from Wai Lin of the Chinese Secret Service.

Stop fidgeting back there...
Turn right. **No – left!** Who's driving?
Bond and Wai Lin

Battling Carver's men in a multi-storey car park, Bond let fly with a missile from the BMW's sunroof battery.

Engine capacity: 5379 cc. **Transmission:** 5-speed automatic **Max. speed:** 155 mph (248 km/h). **Acceleration:** 0-62 mph (0-99 km/h) in 6.8 secs. **Length:** 5.1 m (16 ft 7 in) **Width:** 1.9 m (6 ft 7 in) **Modifications:** rocket battery in sunroof; caltrop dispenser in rear bumper; re-inflatable tyres; smoke and tear gas jets in side trims; chain cutter beneath bonnet badge; electrified door handles; fire-proof and bulletproof body and windows; video link behind driver's mirror to mobile phone controls; spare gun in glove compartment safe.

Do you need collision coverage? **Yes.** Fire? **Probably.**
Property destruction? **Definitely.** Personal injury?
I hope not, but accidents do happen.
They frequently do – with you!

Q and **Bond**

TOUCH
SENSITIVE

Q travelled to Hamburg to present Bond with his "beautiful new car", a BMW 750iL. Not only was the vehicle equipped with an arsenal of gadgets and weapons, it could be driven by remote control. Giving new meaning to the term "backseat driver", Bond employed all the car's functions to make fools of Carver's thugs.

Posing as an Avis car-hire rep, Q explained how to operate the BMW via a pad on Bond's Ericsson mobile phone. The phone's screen showed the driver's view through the windscreen.

EASY RIDERS

Captured and threatened with torture, Bond and Chinese agent Wai Lin escaped Elliot Carver's Saigon headquarters. Handcuffed together, they had little time to figure out how to drive their stolen BMW R1200 bike as the bullets started to fly.

Cornered in a dead end, Bond skidded beneath the whirring blades of one of Carver's helicopters. Then he went on the attack – with a washing line.

The World Is Not Enough ™

A bomb in MI6 headquarters sends Bond tearing up the Thames in Q's latest speedboat. M then dispatches Bond to Azerbaijan to protect the next potential terrorist target, Elektra King of King Industries. Bond discovers that not even his specially modified BMW sports car is enough to escape Elektra's merciless machinations.

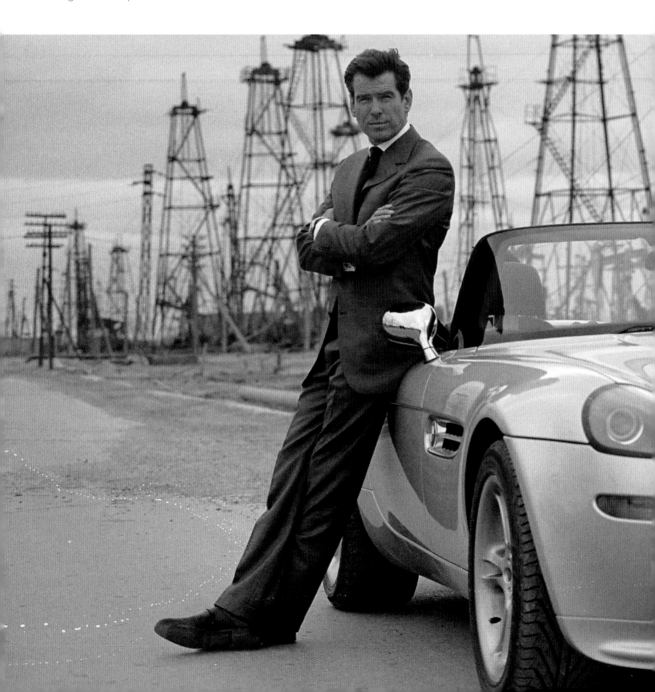

Engine: 5.7-litre V8; 300 Bhp (auxiliary jet engines give extra thrust) **Max. speed:** 100 mph (160 km/h) **Acceleration:** 0-60 mph (0-96 km/h) in 6 secs **Length:** 4.7 m (15 ft 6 in) **Width:** 1.5 m (4 ft 11 in) **Special features:** ejector seat; diving capability; computer port on each side; roll cage; braking chutes in rear compartment; rocket launchers; two smart torpedoes targeted by scanner rangefinder in bow; grenade launchers; twin machine guns.

Q BOAT

A bomb punched a hole in MI6's Thameside HQ. A fusillade of bullets followed, fired by a girl on a Sunseeker launch. Bond seized the only suitable vehicle to catch the assassin – Q's prototype speedboat.

Nothing was going to stand in Bond's way as he pursed the terrorist.

Stop! Stop! It isn't finished!

Q

The Q boat could operate in just a few centimetres of water. With its jet engines at full throttle, Bond also found he could skid the boat down side streets.

119

TORN APART

Parked on a walkway, Bond's gleaming BMW Z8 was a sitting duck. Not even its remote-control capabilities could save it.

Elektra King's treecutting helicopters homed in on Bond when he paid a visit to shady businessman Valentin Zukovsky at his Baku caviar factory. There was little time to talk before the choppers struck – to devastating effect.

A missile from the Z8 downed one helicopter, then Bond had to run for his life as the second chopper's blades carved his car in half.

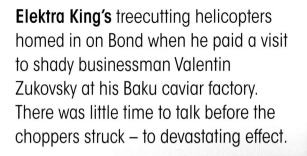

Q's not going to like this!

Bond

Engine: 5.0 litre V8; 4941 cc; 400 bhp **Transmission:** 6-speed manual **Max. speed:** 155 mph (248 km/h) **Acceleration:** 0-62 mph (0-99 km/h) in 4.4 secs **Length:** 4.4 m (14 ft 4in) **Width:** 1.83 m (6 ft 1 in) **Modifications:** radar-guided Stinger missile system in air vents; bulletproof windscreen; remote-control pads in ignition key; "dynamic stability control" to ensure safe handling.

DIE ANOTHER DAY

A mission involving smuggled diamonds and a power-crazed North Korean army officer ends in betrayal, capture and disgrace for Bond. Battling back into M's good books, Bond investigates diamond king Gustav Graves. The industrialist seems to be a flamboyant, speed-loving philanthropist. Bond finds that Graves has another face entirely, some deadly friends and even deadlier dreams.

Warning! Adaptive camouflage failure.
The Aston Martin Vanquish's security system

Bond's assignment in the demilitarized zone between North and South Korea to destroy Colonel Moon's weapons-for-diamonds racket had been betrayed – but that only made him more determined to succeed. Bond seized a hovercraft, used for traversing the mine-infested terrain, and caused chaos in Moon's camp. He then went after Colonel Moon himself.

HOVERCRAFT
HAVOC

Moon discovered that not even his latest toy, a tank-busting gun, could stop Bond's one-man blitz.

ASTON MARTIN VANQUISH

Engine: 5.9 L V12 **Max. speed:** 196 mph (315 km/h) **Acceleration:** 0-62 mph (0-100 km/h) in 4.4 secs **Length:** 4.7 m (15 ft 3 in) **Width:** 1.9 m (6 ft 4 in) **Modifications:** adaptive camouflage system; thermal imaging system; ejector seat; twin target-seeking shotguns in bonnet; twin machine guns and four heat-seeking missiles in grille; spiked tyres for icy conditions; bulletproof windows and body; remote-control console.

The ultimate in British engineering... Aston Martin call it the Vanquish. We call it the "Vanish".

Q

Q handed Bond the car's hefty instruction manual for a couple of hours hard study.

Bond employed the Vanquish's twin target-seeking shotguns to complete his studies in seconds.

In MI6's base in an abandoned London Underground station, Q proudly brought forth Bond's new car. All Bond saw was a flat-bed truck – until Q used the car's key fob to deactivate its "adaptive camouflage" system. The sleek lines of an Aston Martin V12 Vanquish immediately materialized.

He got away.
No matter. The pleasure of the kill is in the chase.

Zao and **Graves**

Bond needed all the ice dragster's 325 mph (521 km/h) to stay ahead of Icarus' conflagrative beams.

ICE DRAGSTER

Thrill-seeker Gustav Graves was proud of his super-fast ice dragster, but now he had bigger fish to fry. When Bond used the dragster to escape Graves' Iceland base, Graves seized the opportunity to test Icarus, his latest, most devastating plaything. This diamond-studded satellite superweapon converted sunlight into a death ray of awesome power.

Dangling over an ice cliff, Bond removed the dragster's rear hatch to parasurf a tidal wave of meltwater.

ZAO'S JAGUAR

Bond had exploded a case of diamonds in Zao's face in the DMZ between North and South Korea and ruined his gene replacement therapy in a Cuban clinic. Graves' henchman longed to get even, and at the wheel of his Jaguar XKR he had the chance to eliminate Bond and have fun doing it.

Zao had the answer to Bond's Aston Martin's adaptive camouflage: a thermal imaging screen. Bullets from the Jag's Gatling gun temporarily disabled Bond's cloaking device.

Zao travelled light – the boot of his XKR was filled by a mortar bomb launch system. Bond destroyed the bombs in mid-air with his car's target-seeking shotguns.

Engine: supercharged 4.0-litre AJ26, giving 400 hp **Max. speed:** 155 mph (249 km/h) **Acceleration:** 0-60 mph (0-96 km/h) in 4.8 secs **Length:** 4.76 m (15 ft 7 in) **Width:** 1.83 m (6 ft) **Modifications:** thermal imaging system; rear-mounted Gatling gun; mortar system in boot; heat-seeking missile battery in grille; twin hydraulic rams in grille.

CASINO ROYALE

007™

James Bond acquires a vintage Aston Martin DB5 in the Bahamas, foils a terrorist plot in Miami, and defeats banker-to-terrorists Le Chiffre at poker in Montenegro. So far, so fair and square – until MI6's new Double-O agent discovers, in the worst possible way, that international espionage is no game and that the players obey no rules.

NASSAU 56526 BAHAMAS

What about a drink at my place?
Your place? Is it close? **Very.**

Bond and Solange

TANKER TERROR

Spurred on by the enigmatic codeword clue "Ellipsis", Bond travelled from Madagascar to the Bahamas and on to Miami tracking a terrorist bomb plot. The target turned out to be the Skyfleet SF70 prototype, the world's largest passenger aircraft. A hijacked fuel tanker was the mobile bomb.

The tanker's brakes failed with Bond at the wheel. To slow the vehicle, he smashed into a line of police cars protecting the aeroplane.

Bond saw Vesper Lynd being bundled into a car and gave chase in his new Aston Martin DBS V12. The car had no special modifications or weapons, but with a top speed of 191 mph (307 km/h), Bond was confident that he would catch Le Chiffre and make him pay. Then Bond's headlights picked out Vesper's body lying in the road. Le Chiffre had left Bond an obstacle he couldn't ignore.

With just a fraction of a second to react, Bond swerved onto a grassy verge. The DBS somersaulted over and over and crashed to a standstill.

ASTON MARTIN DBS

TT - 37B-20

QUANTUM OF SOLACE

With Mr. White secured in his car boot, Bond hopes to get some answers about Vesper Lynd's seeming treachery at the end of their Casino Royale assignment. White escapes, and Bond embarks on a mission of his own to find the truth. With help from Camille, another avenger, Bond exposes a corrupt coup in Latin America and shines a light into the murky dealings of the Quantum organization.

QUARRY CHASE

Bond was driving his Aston Martin DBS with Mr. White in the boot to an MI6 safe house in Siena. The two Alfa Romeo 159s seemed to come out of nowhere, peppering his car with machine-gun fire. Bond was going to have to battle all the way. The first Alfa crashed in heavy traffic near Lake Garda; the second, Bond took for a joy ride through a marble quarry.

72 GH3LD

Missing a door, paintwork covered in quarry dust, the DBS cruised triumphantly into Siena's medieval quarter. Thanks to Bond, White's mysterious organization was down two cars and four assassins.

James Bond will return...

LONDON, NEW YORK, MUNICH,
MELBOURNE AND DELHI

Designed by Dan Bunyan for Dorling Kindersley

Senior Editor Alastair Dougall
Senior Designer Lynne Moulding
Managing Editor Catherine Saunders
Art Director Lisa Lanzarini
Publishing Manager Simon Beecroft
Category Publisher Alex Allan
Production Editor Siu Yin Chan
Production Controller Nick Seston

First published in Great Britain in 2010
by Dorling Kindersley Limited
80 Strand, London, WC2R 0RL

10 11 12 13 10 9 8 7 6 5 4 3 2 1
177922 – 02/10

A CIP catalogue record for this book is available from the British Library

ISBN: 978-1-4053-5535-3

Colour reproduction by Alta Imago, London
Printed and bound in China by Leo Paper Products

Discover more at www.dk.com

The author and Dorling Kindersley would like to thank Jenni McMurrie
of EON Productions for her invaluable help during the production of this book.